For Kids By Kids: Poems About Love

A poetry anthology inspired by love

—Spring 2024—

For Kids By Kids: Poems About Love
© Copyright 2024 Think Ahead Kids Publishing
All rights reserved. No part of this publication may be reproduced, stored in a retrieval system, or transmitted in mechanical, photocopying, recording, or otherwise, without the prior written permission of the copyright owner.
Library of Congress Cataloging-in-Publication Data on file.

Front Cover Art
Star

Back Cover Art
Shya Meza

Copyright Page Art
Shya Meza

Book Design
Amanda Le

Visit ThinkAheadKids.com
Think Ahead Kids Publishing
29910 Murrieta Hot Springs Rd. Suite G226 Murrieta, CA 92563

First Edition

ISBN # 979-8-218-39824-8

CONTENTS

Foreword	4	Veronika Childs
Friends	6	Monika Childs
Unicorn Planet	7	
Moonlight	9	Emily Cunningham
Doggy Bestfriend	11	
Sal's my Pal	13	London Huehmer
Snowflake	14	
Magnificent Pig	15	
Two Pets In A Pod	16	
DOGS	17	Natasha Huehmer
My Sweet Penny	19	
The Best Day	21	Karen Magaña
Milo	22	
Where is Cupid?	23	Savannah Vinci
The ABC's of Love	24	
Creativity	25	Etta Wang
My Opinion	27	
Afterword	29	Marla Huehmer
Acknowledgements	30	
About the Authors	31	
About the Artists	32	

Foreword

The journey of creating this poetry collection began with a simple idea that blossomed into reality through a partnership with the Think Ahead Kids Foundation. Inspired by a shared belief in the power of self-expression through poetry, I embarked on a mission to teach these young writers the art of poetry. It has been my pleasure to witness their growth and creativity throughout our workshop.

Before our class, many of them had never written a poem, yet they embraced the challenge with open hearts and minds, eager to explore their emotions and stories through verse. In this collection, you will find their heartfelt poems, each a testament to their newfound ability to express themselves in a unique and meaningful way. Through their words may you see the wonder and magic of their youth and be inspired to explore your own creativity and embrace the beauty of self-expression through poetry.

To my students: I am immensely proud of your achievements and grateful for the opportunity to be a part of your creative journey. You have inspired me in so many ways, including the poem below.

Carefree days
Hearts of love abound
Illuminated brilliance
Listened to the sound
Did you miss the dance
Here's another chance
Older and older
Over too soon
Dear little one
    soar over the moon

Imagine the stars
New hope in the dark
Never forget
Opus or spark
Creativity composed
Embraced and exposed
Nourish the flame
Cherish each ember
Enjoy every word
    and wonder remembered

Veronika Childs
Children's Book Author & Poet

Artwork by Mya Hill, Age 16

Monika Childs
Age 8

Friends

Fun times
Run and play
Imagine together
Every day
New adventures
Dance with me

Artwork by Ajax Garcia-Hiener, Age 16

Monika Childs
Age 8

Unicorn Planet

I went on adventure to my favorite place
To get there you have to go through space
It's very, very far
Out past the big star
I love unicorns come and see
To unicorn planet, follow me
See the colorful grass and beautiful blooming flowers
Taste the cotton candy clouds and rainbow showers
Fly over the magical mountain
Come taste the chocolate fountain
Cookie houses and chocolate streets
Everything is a treat
Unicorn planet is so much fun
When you play under the warm sun
Unicorn planet is the best
See little ones in their glitter nests?
Listen to their horns make a beautiful sound
Filling the air with laughter all around
I feel happy with my unicorn friends
I wish this dream will never end

Artwork by Monika Childs, Age 8

Emily Cunningham
Age 12

Moonlight

In the quiet of the night,
I hear whispers in the breeze.
I see moonlight dancing through
the trees.
I feel cool air kissing my skin,
I taste the magic,
So serene.

Artwork by Ilianna Villasenor, Age 15

Emily Cunningham
Age 12

Doggy Best Friend

Loyal friend with
a wagging tail.
Offering comfort,
never to fail.
Vivid memories in each
joyful play.
Every bark and cuddle
brightens my day.

Artwork by Star, Age 17

London Huehmer
Age 8

Sal's My Pal

I'm Malibu and here I am
ready to be the star.
I need my car.
Yes, it will be far
but I do not care
because I must
go far for my car.
If I have no car
then the party will have
no Malibu.
I decided I will go
on a caribou.
Yes, I will go
to the party
on a Caribou.
Its name is Sal.
And he is my new Pal.

Artwork by Sophia Alexander, Age 15

London Huehmer
Age 8

Snowflake

Snowflake is my Guinea Pig.
Now what would I do
without you?
Oh Piggy, I love you.
While I give her water
I watch her run.
Full of love is Snowflake.
I love you Snowflake
and I know you love me back.
Kind and cute you are.
Encouraging and fluffy is you.

Artwork by Shya Meza, Age 17

London Huehmer
Age 8

Magnificent Pig

I hear Snowflake squeak.
So, I dash up the stairs
and to her cage.
I see her and my heart melts.
I take off her cage lid
and pick up my perfect Guinea Pig.
I feel her soft fur.
I give her some more food.
I set her back down in her cage.
I see her gulp it down.
This makes me laugh.
I give her a treat.

Artwork by London Huehmer, Age 8

London Huehmer
Age 8

Two Pets In A Pod

You two are my best friends.
Your pelts are so fluffy.
You are my Pup and
You are my Little Guinea Pig.
Pup, you are gray and white.
Guinea Pig you are all white.
Yet you two are not polar opposites.
Your eyes are round and cute.
My dear puppy, you are the best.
The most adorable, awesome, beautiful,
trustworthy doggy friend ever.
My dear Guinea Pig, you are the best, awesome,
beautiful, and trustworthy Guinea Pig friend ever.
I love you two with all my heart.
You Are my Two Pets in a Pod.

Artwork by London Huehmer, Age 8

Natasha Huehmer
Age 13

DOGS

Determined to get that treat.
One of kind and neat.
Grateful for you.
Smart, it's true.

Artwork by Mya Hill, Age 16

Natasha Huehmer
Age 13

My Sweet Penny

You were just eight weeks old
when we first met.
I saw you sitting on the grass,
all happy and playful.
I know you were the puppy
I was meant to get.
Your fur was so soft
and scruffy.
Your eyes were clear
and brown.
You were way cuter
than any stuffy.
I picked you up
and held you tight.
You licked my cheek and barked.
I knew you were right.

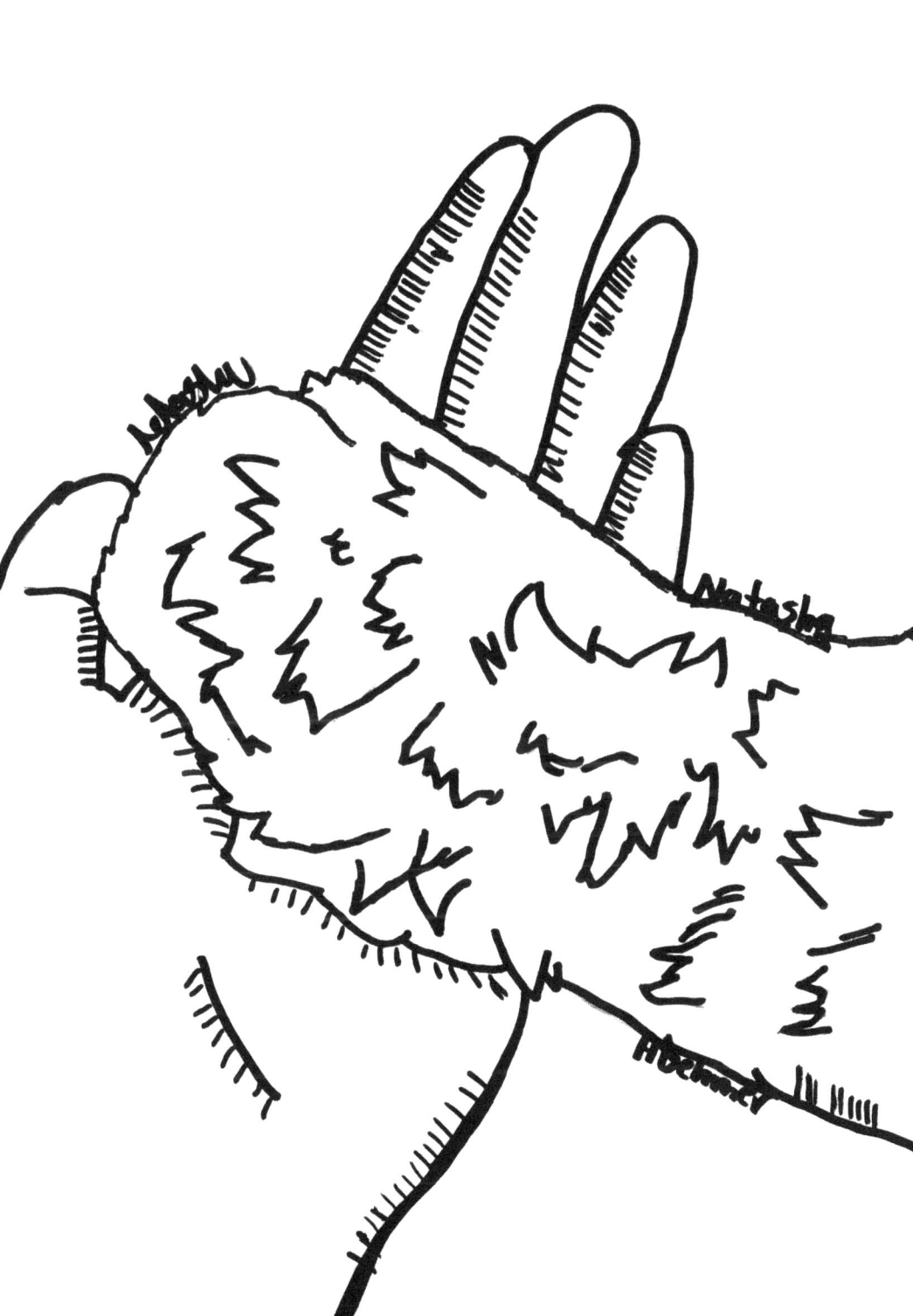

Karen Magaña
Age 8

The Best Day

On a boring rainy day
my sister and I wanted to play.
We couldn't go outside
but I had my dog by my side.
He has the cutest eyes
and the fluffiest coat.
All day we colored on his coat.
He looked beautiful
when he was finished.
And when the rain went away
we played outside.
We turned a boring day
into a fun time

Artwork by Ajax Garcia-Hiener, Age 16

Karen Magaña
Age 8

Milo

My fluffy canine
I love you so much.
Lucky for me
    you were chosen to be mine.
Only with you
    I will share my lunch.

Artwork by Karen Magaña, Age 8

Savannah Vinci
Age 11

Where is Cupid?

I see people hugging all around me.
I feel a little lonely but also happy.
I smell the fresh flowers that people have received.
I feel kind of lonely sitting on the street.

Artwork by Sophia Alexander, Age 15

Savannah Vinci
Age 11

The ABC's of Love

Lifting
Out of the box
Very kind
Extra caring
Helpful
Extraordinary
Affection
Respectful
Thoughtful

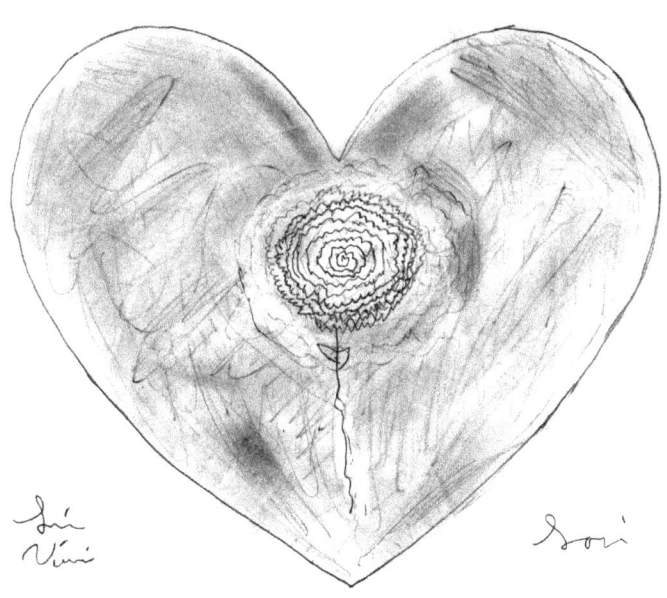

Artwork by Savannah Vinci, Age 11

Etta Wang
Age 11

Creativity

I see someone coming alive on paper.
I hear my friends encouraging me while my pencil
sketches and scratches.
I taste my hair falling into my face.
I feel the paper filled with color.
I smell the strong scent of a sharpie while I work.
I feel focused as my creative sense flows.
Filled with details, my paper glows.

Artwork by Joseph Lockhart, Age 17

Etta Wang
Age 11

My Opinion

Doing art is what is fun.
Rubbing pastels.
And adding colors.
When I draw, I scritch and sketch.
In my head, things I see,
nothing can compare to them.
So, I get a pencil to illustrate them.

Artwork by Etta Wang, age 11

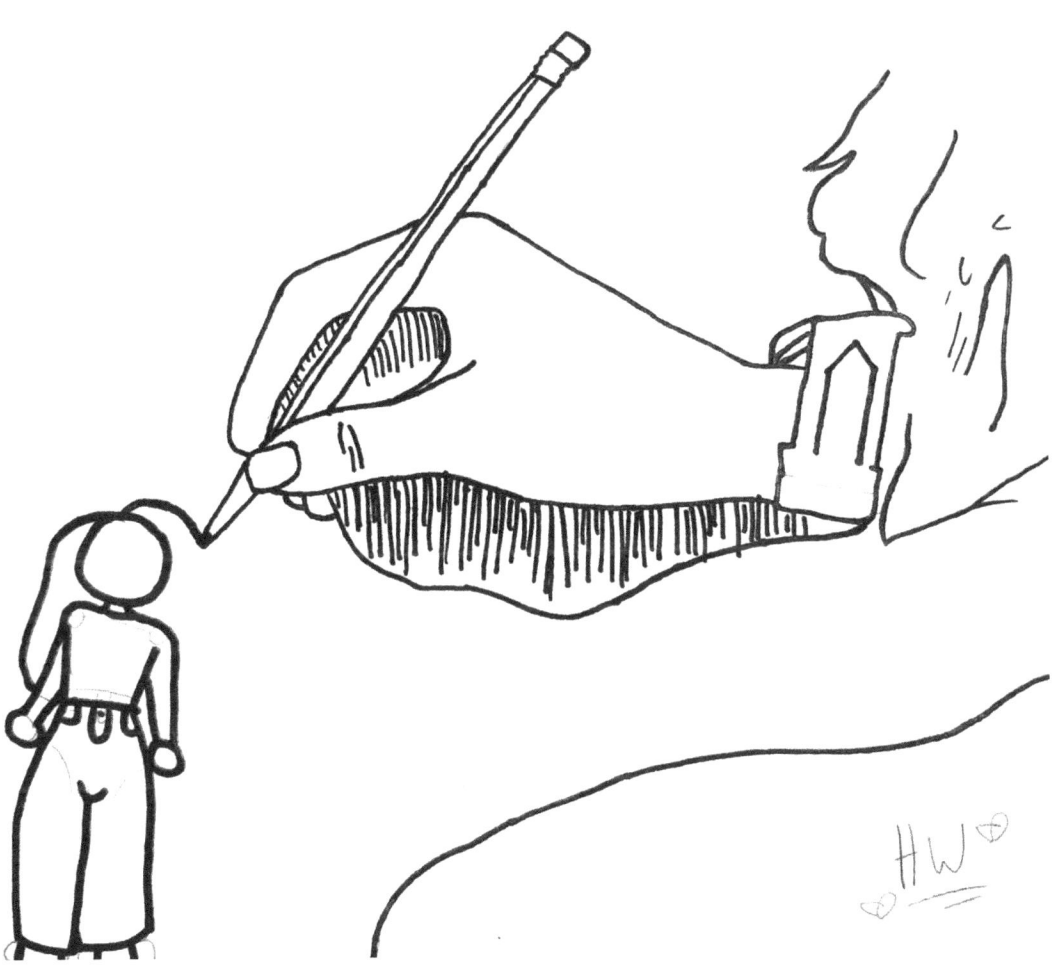

Afterword

It's not every day that a child writes and publishes a book. When such a remarkable event occurs, it's a true testament to that child's passion, dedication, and talent. In the case of these young authors, *For Kids By Kids: Poems About Love* exemplifies the astonishing ability of young minds when they put their creativity into motion.

This book was made possible by the generous support of the Think Ahead Kids Foundation and its donors. The foundation focuses on fulfilling the dreams of young writers by raising funds to publish child authors. Through Think Ahead Kids Publishing, each child's story is carefully edited and illustrated with professional assistance, allowing their creativity to blossom on the pages of a real book. The foundation's commitment to nurturing the creativity of children enables young authors to bring their imaginative tales to life in published form. With the help of donations, the Think Ahead Kids Foundation can make many children's dreams of becoming published authors come true.

Marla Huehmer
Founder
Think Ahead Kids Foundation

Acknowledgements

The Think Ahead Kids Foundation extends its heartfelt gratitude to the following individuals and organizations whose support has made the publication of this book possible. To join us as a patron, visit thinkaheadkidsfoundation.org or, for more information, email info@thinkaheadkidsfoundation.org.

Patrons
Cindy Magaña
Nicole Merete
Abra Vegter Wang
Starbucks Foundation

We would like to thank *Tony Moramarco* for allowing us to use his studio space and collaborating with Think Ahead Kids on the completion of this anthology, as well as the students of *Bigfoot Art Classes* who have contributed their beautiful artworks to the poems and the cover design of this book.

Veronika Childs has been invaluable in teaching the art of poetry to the students and giving the students another beautiful way to express themselves through their writing. Veronika took on a brand new challenge by volunteering her time to teach a subject she has been passionate about since she was young. We are proud to see her be able to share her passion with blooming creatives.

Amanda Le has volunteered their time and effort between projects to design this book, formatting, and the completion of this anthology project. With their high standard for art and design, they helped immensely to deliver a beautiful result with high quality works made entirely by the students.

About the Authors

Monika Childs is an 8-year-old living in Southern California. She is known for her curiosity, creativity, and boundless energy. Monika loves drawing pictures and writing short stories and poems. When she grows up, she aspires to be a writer, an artist, and a scientist.

Emily Cunningham is a 12-year-old girl who loves expressing herself through art and uses her drawings to capture her feelings. Emily has been writing for some time now and has published a book about a pirate.

London Huehmer is an 8-year-old who loves to read and write stories. She is a proud member of the MENSA High IQ Society. She is one of the founders of the Think Ahead Kids Foundation. Writing takes her away to a place where she can create characters and settings focused on magical adventures. When she is not reading or writing, London also enjoys training her puppies, playing the piano and singing.

Natasha Huehmer has published Beginner Reader books titled Puppy's Garden Adventure (English and Spanish editions) and Puppy's Beach Adventure, as well as Puppy's Garden Adventure Coloring and Activity Story Book. She is the Co-Founder of Think Ahead Kids Foundation and works diligently interviewing inspirational people with her sister to inspire young minds. She enjoys walking her dogs, swimming, going to the beach, and writing! Find her work at thinkaheadkids.com

Karen Magaña is an 8-year-old and is local to Southern California. She loves to read, paint and draw.

Savannah Vinci is an 11-year-old local to Southern California. She loves to express her creative side through writing short stories, songs, and poems. Savannah loves writing because it allows her to use her ideas to create characters and storylines that other people can relate to.

Etta Wang is an 11-year-old Asian-American girl that enjoys drawing people, singing, and making funny videos as well as hanging out with her besties. Etta is passionate about writing because, as she puts it, "it can be anything you can imagine or create!" She has been honing her writing skills for about two years, starting in third grade. Etta's first picture book, *The Pig Hairstylist*, is set to be published in the autumn of 2024.

About the Artists

Sophia Alexander is a 15-year-old artist who loves animation and cartooning. She also loves creating characters and costumes. Drawing has been a part of her life for as long as she can remember, and she aspires to pursue a career as an animator.

Shya Meza is a 17-year-old artist from Southern California. Shya finds joy in creating art, particularly in drawing her own original characters, and designing tattoo concepts that often adorn these characters. She has been dedicated to drawing for about five years and has showcased her talent in several art contests, including Cartoonapalooza in 2023 where she won a first-place award. For more of Shya's work, visit @darkie_sharkie007 on Instagram.

Ajax Garcia-Hiener is a cartoonist and an artist. He often draws animals. For more of Ajax's work, go to @free_wolfx on Instagram.

Mya Hill is an artist who loves making her and other's visions come to life. Drawing has been a lifelong passion for her. For more of Mya's work, visit @sparklydragondreamer on Instagram.

Joseph Lockhart is a 17-year-old artist who resides in Southern California. He started drawing to pass the time and realized he enjoyed the process of conveying his ideas on paper. Joseph has been causally drawing for 9 years and this book is his first officially published piece.

Star, a 17-year-old artist, discovered her love for art as a child by drawing her favorite cat characters from books. Star specializes in cartoon animals as well as semi-realistic animal portraits. She has honed her skills through art classes with Bigfoot's Art Studio alongside advanced placement art classes through her high school. Beyond her artistic pursuits, Star has found a sense of belonging and community through art and creative spaces.

Ilianna Villasenor is a 15-year-old artist, and she has enjoyed art all her life. Her artistic journey has already seen remarkable achievements, such as being displayed at the Temecula Museum, and being sold to a business owner to be used as a logo. Iliana's art has been featured in 2 books.

Also Available from Think Ahead Kids

Wings to Fly by Lydia Wallis, Illustrated by Amanda Le (2023)

Puppy's Beach Adventure by Natasha Huehmer, Illustrated by Dori Durbin (2023)

La Aventura de la Perrita en el Jardin (Spanish Edition to Puppy's Garden Adventure) by Natasha Huehmer, Illustrated by Dori Durbin (2022)

Puppy's Garden Adventure Coloring and Activity Storybook by Natasha Huehmer, Illustrated by Dori Durbin (2022)

Puppy's Garden Adventure by Natasha Huehmer, Illustrated by Dori Durbin (2022)

The Big Move by Marla Huehmer, Illustrated by Marla Huehmer, Natahsa Huehmer, and London Huehmer (2020)

www.ingramcontent.com/pod-product-compliance
Lightning Source LLC
LaVergne TN
LVHW051034070526
838201LV00009B/196